Festivals *of the* World

MONGOLIA

Gareth Stevens Publishing
MILWAUKEE

Written by
FREDERICK FISHER

Edited by
GERALDINE MESENAS

Designed by
HASNAH MOHD ESA

Picture research by
SUSAN JANE MANUEL

First published in North America in 1999 by
Gareth Stevens Publishing
1555 North RiverCenter Drive, Suite 201
Milwaukee, Wisconsin 53212 USA

For a free color catalog describing Gareth
Stevens' list of high-quality books and multimedia
programs, call
1-800-542-2595 (USA)
or 1-800-461-9120 (Canada).
Gareth Stevens Publishing's Fax: (414) 225-0377.
See our catalog, too, on the World Wide Web:
http://gsinc.com

© **TIMES EDITIONS PTE LTD 1999**
Originated and designed by
Times Books International
an imprint of Times Editions Pte Ltd
Times Centre, 1 New Industrial Road
Singapore 536196
Printed in Singapore

Library of Congress Cataloging-in-Publication Data:
Fisher, Frederick.
Mongolia / by Frederick Fisher.
p. cm.—(Festivals of the world)
Includes bibliographical references and index.
Summary: Describes how the culture of Mongolia
is reflected in its many festivals, including the
Obo Shrine Festival, Naadam Festival,
and Tsagaan Sar.
ISBN 0-8368-2024-X (1ib. bdg.)
1. Festivals—Mongolia—Juvenile literature.
2. Mongolia—Social life and customs—Juvenile
literature. [1. Festivals—Mongolia. 2. Holidays—
Mongolia. 3. Mongolia—Social life and customs.]
I. Title. II. Series.
GT4886.M65F57   1999
394.26951'7—dc21   98-39808

1 2 3 4 5 6 7 8 9 03 02 01 00 99

CONTENTS

It's Festival Time . . .

Mongolians love to celebrate for any reason at all, and the Mongolian calendar is filled with religious and national holidays. Mongolians celebrate with lots of food, music played on traditional instruments, and traditional dancing. Cheer as boys and girls race each other in the *Naadam* [NAH-dahm] horse races and learn how a *ger* [GAIR] is set up. Watch the colorful and spectacular *Tsam* [SAHM} mask dance and learn to make *banch* [BAHN-chuh]. Smile! It's festival time in Mongolia!

WHERE'S MONGOLIA?

Mongolia is sandwiched between China and Russia. It is divided into two countries—Inner Mongolia, which is part of China, and Outer Mongolia, an **independent republic** and the country to which this book refers.

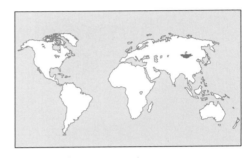

Mongolia's capital city is Ulaanbaatar. The country has many lakes and a large desert, called the Gobi Desert. Nomads, people who travel from place to place, live on Mongolia's flat grasslands, called steppes.

Who are the Mongolians?

Mongolian ancestors were known as the Hun of Attila. They were fierce fighters and conquered parts of Europe. The most famous Mongolian is Genghis Khan. He ruled Mongolia in 1206 and conquered many lands for the Mongolian Empire.

Mongolia has very few people in proportion to land size. Mongolians make up 70 percent of the population. The next largest group (only 6 percent) are Turks. The rest are small groups of Chinese and Russians. The people's basic language is Cyrillic, the same language Russians use.

Left: A little Mongolian boy practices roping horses.

Opposite: The small town of Buyant in Western Mongolia.

MONGOLIA

RUSSIA

Mörön●   Darhan●

Erdenet●   ●ULAANBAATAR

Altai Range   *Hangayn Nuruu*

●Buyant   ●Karakorum

Gobi Desert

INNER MONGOLIA

N

PEOPLES REPUBLIC
OF CHINA

WHEN'S THE PARTY?

The Mongolians find reasons to celebrate all year round, for marriages, birthdays, anniversaries, and other occasions. They make a holiday out of setting up a new ger and have a **lavish** party for a baby's first haircut! Mongolians even have holidays devoted to milkmaids and herders!

Join me and other colorfully dressed people in the Naadam parade on page 20.

AUTUMN & WINTER

- ✪ **FESTIVAL OF FIRE**—Celebrated in autumn, on the first day of the eighth lunar month.
- ✪ **MONGOLIAN REPUBLIC DAY**—Celebrated on November 26th.
- ✪ **GREAT SACRIFICIAL FEAST TO THE FIRE GOD**
- ✪ **CHRISTMAS**—Mongolia's Christmas celebrations are filled with glitzy lights, beautiful decorations, Father Christmas, and trees.
- ✪ **TSAGAAN SAR**—Mongolia's national Lunar New Year is celebrated in February, on the first day of spring according to the lunar calendar. It is a family event.

6

It's really cold in Mongolia, and we are all bundled up to have fun in the snow!

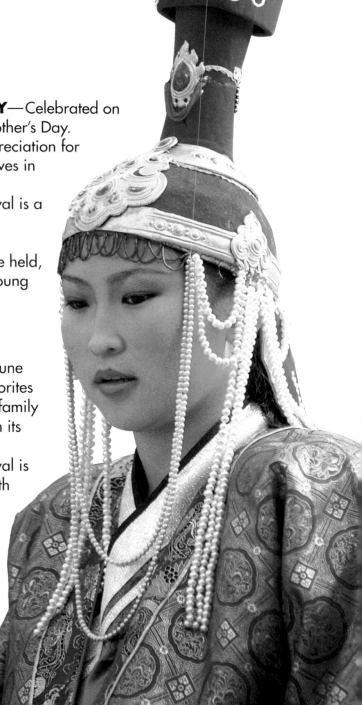

SPRING

- **INTERNATIONAL WOMAN'S DAY**—Celebrated on March 8th, this holiday is similar to Mother's Day. Husbands and children show their appreciation for mothers, grandmothers, sisters, and wives in many different ways.
- **OBO SHRINE FESTIVAL**—This festival is a religious celebration that is a lot of fun, especially toward the end of the day. Wrestling and archery competitions are held, as well as a race in which the tribes' young men ride their best horses.

SUMMER

- **CHILDREN'S DAY**—Celebrated on June 1st, this day is one of the children's favorites because they receive many gifts. Each family has its own gathering and celebrates in its own way.
- **MIDSUMMER FESTIVAL**—This festival is celebrated on the twelfth day of the sixth lunar month.
- **NATIONAL DAY**—This holiday is celebrated on July 11th.
- **NAADAM FESTIVAL**
- **TSAM**

NOMADIC FESTIVALS

Nomads make up about one-third of the total Mongolian population. They live in tents, called gers, and lead a wandering lifestyle that revolves around their cattle. They constantly move as they search for pastures and water for their cattle. Nomads lead a hard life, but they are happy people and celebrate all year round. They even have feasts in honor of herders, milkmaids, and horses! Read on to find out how to celebrate Mongolian-style!

The door of the ger is usually small and brightly colored.

The ger's sides are covered with animal skins in winter.

Festival of the new ger

Building a new ger is a time to celebrate, and everybody joins in. The ger's design has been developed for generations to suit the needs of its **inhabitants**. It is warm in winter, yet cool in summer. It is **collapsible** and can be set up again in an hour.

Lattice walls are formed by criss-crossing wooden poles and tying them with leather thongs. Roof poles are like beams in any house, connecting the sides with the top. Doors are small, so you have to stoop to get in.

There is lots of laughter as the party puts the jigsaw pieces of the ger together. There is lots of food and drink, too, and everyone has a good time.

Above: A ger is a nomad's home. It is divided into separate living spaces, with a living room, kitchen, and bedroom.

Mongolian nomads live in gers year round and prefer them to other forms of housing.

Herders' festivals

Nomads celebrate many holidays that have to do with their herds. The nomads' livelihood depends entirely on their cattle, so there is cause for celebration when a little calf or foal is delivered. Nomads also have days dedicated to herders and milkmaids.

The birth of a calf is an exciting event for a nomad. Healthy calves mean herds will grow. Horse breeding is an especially big event because Mongolian ponies are treasured animals.

Parties usually start at sundown, at the flattest part of the campsite. Nomads celebrate with lots of feasting and music.

Above: The Tsaatan people live in northern Mongolia. Their **existence** is based on reindeer, which provide them with milk, meat, transportation, and skins for clothing and tents.

Nomadic children learn to care for animals at a very young age.

Mongolian music

Music is at the heart of every Mongolian festival. Traditional Mongolian folk instruments are still used today. They include wind instruments, string instruments, and drums made out of python skin or stretched animal skin. The most famous Mongolian instrument is the *morin khuur* [MO-reen KOOR]. It is a beautifully decorated two-stringed lute with a carving of a horse's head at the top. When the music starts, if you listen close enough, you might even hear the famous Mongolian throat singing!

Think about this

Horses are a very important form of transportation for Mongolian nomads. Mongolian children learn to ride horses as early as 18 months old, and they become accomplished riders at a very young age. Children also are often involved in breaking in, or taming, wild horses.

Top and left: Music is a very important part of any Mongolian festival. Even Western instruments have been adopted by the Mongolians (see picture at the top.) Notice the traditional morin khuur with the horse's head carving in the picture on the left.

TSAGAAN SAR

I t's New Year's time. *Tsagaan Sar* [TSAH-gahn SAHR], or White Month, is the Mongolian Lunar New Year. It is celebrated on the first day of spring. Tsagaan Sar is still celebrated the traditional way—Mongolian families visit each other and honor the elders.

Shakyamuni

On the first day of Tsagaan Sar, lamas, or Buddhist monks, greet each other and say prayers to mark the beginning of the new year. During the following 15 days, they hold divine services celebrating the 15 miracles accomplished by *Shakyamuni* [SHOCK-yah-moo-knee], or Buddha. Lamas pray for the protection of nature. They also pray for the people—for their happiness, long life, and help for their problems.

Left: Children often become lamas at an early age and spend a lifetime in the robes.

Opposite: The place where lamas live and pray is called a monastery. This picture shows lamas chanting and praying in a Buddhist temple.

A Mongolian family visiting the capital, Ulaanbaatar, on New Year's Day in their new coats and fur caps.

New Year's Day

On New Year's Day, every Mongolian wakes up and asks, "Have you slept well?" They do not wish each other a "Happy New Year" like we do. Everybody puts on a new cap to signify a good start for the year. The caps are made of fur, with yellow silk linings and flaps covering the ears and back of the neck.

Every Mongolian ger has an altar decorated with butter lamps, or small brass cups filled with butter. The altar stands almost exactly opposite the door. Upon entering a ger, New Year's Day visitors turn first to the altar and worship. After worshiping, they may talk to the host and other guests in the tent.

When visiting each other's ger, Mongolians bow and ask, " Have we not embraced yet?" The answer is, "It is now time." They embrace each other saying, "*Sain-O?* [sane-OH]", meaning "Are you well?" The embrace is a simple gesture. Two people stretch out their arms toward each other and touch elbows. Mongolians shake elbows, not hands.

A typical Mongolian altar, with a butter lamp and pictures of Genghis Khan and lamas.

The feasting begins!

After embracing, the New Year's feast begins. Guests eat from a plate containing bread, fruits, and roasted millet, or grains. A Mongolian delicacy served during the new year is banch, or lamb dumplings. Chinese wine is served, as well as a drink called *airag* [AH-rag], made from mare's milk and a glob of butter, and usually served warm from a thermos bottle.

After eating their fill, guests move on to the next ger to repeat the same ceremony. When people go visiting on New Year's Day, they must hurry. It is important to get back to one's own ger to receive visitors.

Think about this

The lama is a spiritual leader like a priest or a rabbi. Some lamas are considered to be **reincarnations** of powerful spiritual leaders that lived a long time ago. Do you know of any other religions with followers that believe in reincarnation? What are they?

A Mongolian couple preparing a pot of airag for the new year celebrations.

FAMILY FESTIVALS

Mongolians have wonderful celebrations with their families. The nomads, especially, have close-knit family units because they live and work together so far out on the steppes. Many of these family celebrations are familiar to us and are similar to other international celebrations. Two such family national holidays are Woman's Day and Children's Day.

Mongolian women

Mongolian women, especially nomads, work very hard. Because nomads live in gers and move several times a year, they do not have the modern **amenities** to which we are accustomed, such as washing machines and electric ovens. Daily chores, therefore, can be hard, exhausting work.

Preparing a simple meal can be a long and tiring process. There are no supermarkets from which to buy meat and milk. The women themselves have to kill animals for meat. To get the dairy products Mongolians especially enjoy, the women milk the animals daily and make cream, cheese, and yogurt from the milk.

Mongolian women milk the animals daily to make dairy products.

Woman's Day

Woman's Day is a celebration of all women. This national holiday is observed on March 8th and is very much like Mother's Day.

Above: With her long list of daily chores, a Mongolian woman must also look after the herds.

Mothers, grandmothers, aunts, daughters, and female cousins are honored on Woman's Day. Men and children show their appreciation by showering their female relatives with gifts and doing favors for them throughout the day.

Woman's Day is a wonderful way for fathers, sons, and brothers to say "Thank you."

Holding the tail out of Mother's way as she milks the cow!

17

A child's life

Mongolian children start working hard and learn how to take care of animals at an early age. Many are herders at the age of eight or ten and are responsible for taking care of the cattle as they graze. Although the cattle often graze far from the family ger, these children stay with the herds and sleep in the open. Mongolian children must attend school, but many of them still have to do daily chores. Parents realize how hard their children work, so on Children's Day, no chores—only fun!

Children's Day

Every year, on June 1st, Mongolian families plan a big day for their children. Shows and plays are performed in the cities especially for young people. Most of the children like to go to amusement parks, with merry-go-rounds and other thrilling rides.

For Children's Day, parents make or buy all the snack foods their children like best, such as candy, ice cream, dried curds, melted cream with raisins, dried cheese, and other dairy products. It is no wonder, then, that this is the favorite day of the year for Mongolian children!

Opposite: Amusement parks are children's favorite places, with lots of exciting rides to try.

Think about this

A favorite activity of Mongolian children is horseback riding. Whenever they can, Mongolian children practice riding for the horse races in the annual Naadam festival (see pages 20-23). They also love roping horses and racing each other on horses and camels.

A proud Mongolian father and his two young children.

NAADAM FESTIVAL

All of Mongolia plans ahead each year for its most exciting holiday: Naadam Festival, or The Three Games of Men. It begins each year on National Day (July 11th) and is held for three days in all Mongolian provinces and counties.

Warriors on parade

The most spectacular celebration occurs at Mongolia's capital city, Ulaanbaatar. The festival starts with an elaborate ceremony, in which hundreds of military soldiers march to warlike music. The soldiers are followed by men in traditional warrior costumes and colorful monks and athletes on parade. There is lots of music and dancing.

Over the next three days, horse racing, wrestling, and archery competitions take place. These are the three traditional skills of Mongolia. Other exciting performances include acrobatic stunts, parachute jumps, and motorcycle shows.

Left and top: Children are not left out of the Naadam festivities. In fact, children are the main participants in the horse races.

Above: As many as 1,500 children take part in the horse racing competition. This picture shows the winners doing a victory lap.

Horse racing

The horse racing competititon is the most exciting part of the festivities. All competitors are boys and girls between the ages of five and twelve. They are highly skilled riders and wear fancy ornamental costumes. The Naadam horse races are usually 16.7 miles (27 kilometers) across rough country.

Winners ride three victory laps led by a man who shouts a poem about the **virtues** of the horse, the rider, and the owner. An interesting tradition is that riders who lose are also rewarded and honored. Spectators shout encouragement to them as they are led up to the main stand.

The grand festival makes everyone remember how great the Mongol warriors once were.

A Mongolian wrestler must not only be strong but must also have perfect technique. Most important is an ability to twist the body around. The first wrestler to force a rival to kneel on the ground or to touch the ground with an elbow is the winner.

Wrestling

Wrestling contests take place in the center of a large, grassy plain. Several hundred rivals enter the field, each dressed in a special brightly colored, tight-fitting costume, known as the *Dzodog Shudag* [ZOH-dog SHOE-dag], and ornamental kneeboots. It is a fabulous sight. The contests are conducted with the same great ceremony that was practiced hundreds of years ago. A wrestler extends his arms, imitating the flight of the mythical Garuda bird, then performs the traditional eagle's dance, which symbolizes power and **invincibility**. The wrestler who is the final winner at Naadam becomes a national hero.

Mongolians are very **accomplished** wrestlers, and wrestling is one of the few events in which they participate at the Olympic Games every four years.

Little boys practice their wrestling technique.

Think about this
The bow and arrow have been used in Mongolia for thousands of years to hunt animals that provide food for the family. In ancient times, scouts often sent messages from the top of a mountain to a station far below by wrapping the messages around arrows.

Archers range from the very old to the very young in the Naadam festivities.

Archery

Both men and women, young and old, compete at the Naadam archery competitions. Everyone dresses up in a fancy, colorful national costume, called *del* [DEL]. Even children wear the del and look very grown up.

Mongolians use a bow made of layers of horn, sinew, bark, and wood. Crowds looking on appreciate the archers' skill and respect this ancient sport. The arrow is difficult to see when it is first released because it flies through the air so swiftly. Markers sing out "*Punkhai* [punk-HI]!" as the arrow speeds toward the target. When the arrow lands, a marker signals the accuracy of the shot, and the crowd cheers.

Arrows are aimed at a row of woven leather rings laid out together on the ground. Men shoot about 40 arrows and must score at least 15 points, while women shoot 20 arrows and have to score at least 13 points.

TSAM

T sam is an ancient ritual mask dance. According to legend, it was created more than a thousand years ago in Tibet by a god named *Padmasambhava* [PAHD-mah-SAHM-buh-hava], who was famous for defeating demons and evil spirits.

The masks

Lamas introduced Tsam to Mongolia in the 16th century. The costumes and masks of the Mongolian Tsam are boldly colored in red, black, yellow, white, and blue, and they look very fierce and expressive. Masks are double life size and very bright, so the audience can see them clearly. Lamas direct the rituals and make sure the masks are made according to ancient rules. The Tsam masks usually are expertly made and elaborately decorated. Respect for the gods the masks represent is very important. Artists create the masks from papier-mâché and use coral, gold, silver, and precious stones for eyes, collars, and rich designs.

This elaborate mask of *Yamaradja* [YAH-mah-ra-ja], the Lord of Hades, is topped with a crown of skulls.

The battle between good and evil

Above: A colorful, spectacular Tsam dance, depicting the triumph of good over evil.

The actors, dressed in huge, grotesque masks, perform ancient ritual dances and scenes from the lives of heaven-dwellers and heroes. By their movements and gestures, they convey the idea of the eternal **triumph** of good over evil and life over death. These are not speaking parts; they are more like **mime**. Acting out the silent parts takes a great deal of talent. Wearing their huge, colorful masks, these actors leap about the stage performing a **dynamic** dance.

Some of the Tsam masks are stored at the beautiful Erdene Zuu Monastery in Karakorum.

25

THINGS FOR YOU TO DO

C hess is a popular game in Mongolia. Wood sculptors and stone carvers make wonderful chess pieces, often carving figurines from sandalwood or ivory in the shapes of whatever they want. The chess pieces might be lions, tigers, fast horses, fierce-looking camels, warriorlike women, horse-drawn carts, castles, or a king seated on a throne. Read on and learn to make a Mongolian chess set!

What you will need

Each chess piece will be a symbol of something Mongolian, such as a person, animal, or object that you have seen or read about. Before you start making your chess set, ask your parents or a teacher to show you how to play chess. Many schools have chess clubs.

To make the chess pieces, you will need colored pencils, scissors, glue, a ruler, modeling clay, and eight notecards—3 inches x 5 inches (7.5 centimeters x 12.5 centimeters)—four cards of one color and four cards of another color. To make the chess board, you will need a 16-inch (40-cm) square of white cardboard. Get everything ready and start making your very own Mongolian chess set.

Make a Mongolian chess set

For the chess pieces, cut the notecards exactly in half each way to get four oblong cards. You should have 16 oblong cards for each color. Now, decide what shapes you want your chess pieces to be. The standard chess set has the following pieces for each color: one king, one queen, two bishops, two knights, two rooks (or castles), and eight pawns. Look at the pictures in this book or check the library for books with pictures of Mongolian people, animals, or characters. Some suggestions are Genghis Khan, lamas, camels, horses, archers, wrestlers, gers, tigers, or lions.

Once you have decided on the shapes, draw them vertically on the oblong cards. You need two sets of identical drawings for each character—one set of each color. Then, cut out the figures, carefully push them into small blocks of modeling clay, and let the clay harden.

For the chess board, make eight markings, 2 inches (5 cm) apart, along each side of the square of white cardboard. Connect the markings on each side with the ones directly opposite to make 64 squares. Each square should measure 2 inches x 2 inches (5 cm x 5 cm). Color every alternate square black, starting with a square in the corner.

Now you have your own Mongolian chess set! If you like, you can even play checkers on it!

Things to look for in your library

Cowboy on the Steppes. Song Nan Zhang (Tundra Publishing, 1997).
Folktales of Mongolia. B. Khurebat and Aditya Narain (Sterling Publications, 1992).
The Khan's Daughter: A Mongolian Folktale. Laurence Yep (Scholastic Paperbacks, 1997).
The Land and People of Mongolia. *Portraits of Nations* (series). John S. Major (Lippincott-Raven Publishing, 1990).
Mongolia. *Enchantment of the World* (series). Marlene Targ-Brill (Children's Book Press, 1992).
Mongolia: Vanishing Cultures. *Vanishing Cultures* (series). Jan Reynolds (Harcourt Brace, 1994).
Mongolian Folktales. Hilary Roe Metternich, ed. (Avery Press, 1996).

MAKE A GER

ongolian nomads live on the steppes and move several times a year to find better pasture and water for their cattle. The ger is an ideal form of housing for them. It is cheap, collapsible, and easy to transport. Follow the simple steps below to make your own Mongolian ger!

2

3

5

4

6

1

7

You will need:
1. Thin cardboard, 15" x 21" (38 x 53 cm)
2. Ruler
3. Black wax pencil
4. Glue
5. Compass
6. Scissors
7. A piece of cloth, 16" x 22" (40 x 55 cm)

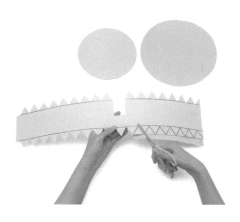

1 Glue the cloth onto the cardboard. With a compass, draw two circles on the cardboard, one 7" (18 cm) across and one 9" (23 cm) across, and cut them out. Draw and cut out a 5" x 21" (13 cm x 53 cm) rectangle. Draw a line 1" (2.5 cm) from each edge along the two long sides of the rectangle, then draw in zigzag lines (as shown in the picture.) Cut out the triangles to make a zigzag pattern along each edge. Cut a small rectangle in the middle of one edge to make the door of the ger.

2 Draw a straight line from the edge of the bigger circle to its center. Cut along the line. Then, overlap the two corners to make a cone (see picture) and glue the two sides together. Glue the two ends of the rectangle together, also.

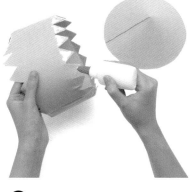

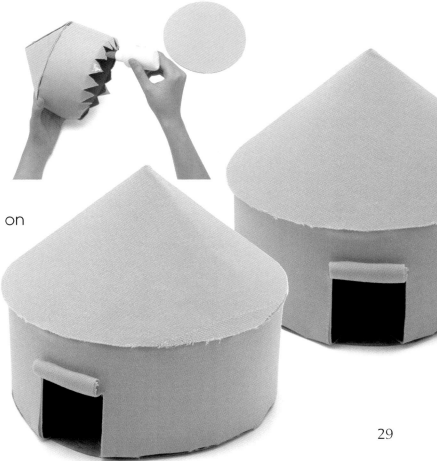

3 Glue along the zigzag edge of the rectangle on the side without the door and attach the cone— this is the roof. Glue along the other zigzag edge and attach the smaller circle to make the base of the ger. Now you have your very own Mongolian ger!

MAKE BANCH

O ne of the Mongolians' favorite meat dishes is banch, or steamed lamb dumplings. You can also make this delicious dish with beef, as we have done here. Follow the simple steps below to prepare this Mongolian treat!

You will need:
1. 8 oz. (230 g) flour
2. 5 fl. oz. (150 ml) cold water
3. 1 teaspoon of pepper
4. 1 teaspoon of salt
5. Measuring spoons
6. 8 oz. (230 g) raw ground beef
7. A mixing bowl
8. A chopping board
9. 3 oz. (90 g) chopped cabbage
10. 3 oz. (90 g) chopped onions
11. A spoon
12. A wooden spoon
13. A rolling pin

1 Mix the beef, onions, and cabbage together in the mixing bowl. Add salt and pepper to the mixture.

2 Mix flour and cold water to make a soft dough. Let the dough sit for 10 minutes.

3 Roll small lumps of dough into thin circles, each with a diameter of about 3" (7.5 cm). The dough circles should be thin at the edges and thicker in the middle.

4 Drop a tablespoon of the meat and vegetable mixture onto each circle of dough. Fold the edges over the mixture to form a flowerlike pattern. Ask your parents to steam the dumplings for 20 minutes. Now you have a pretty Mongolian snack!

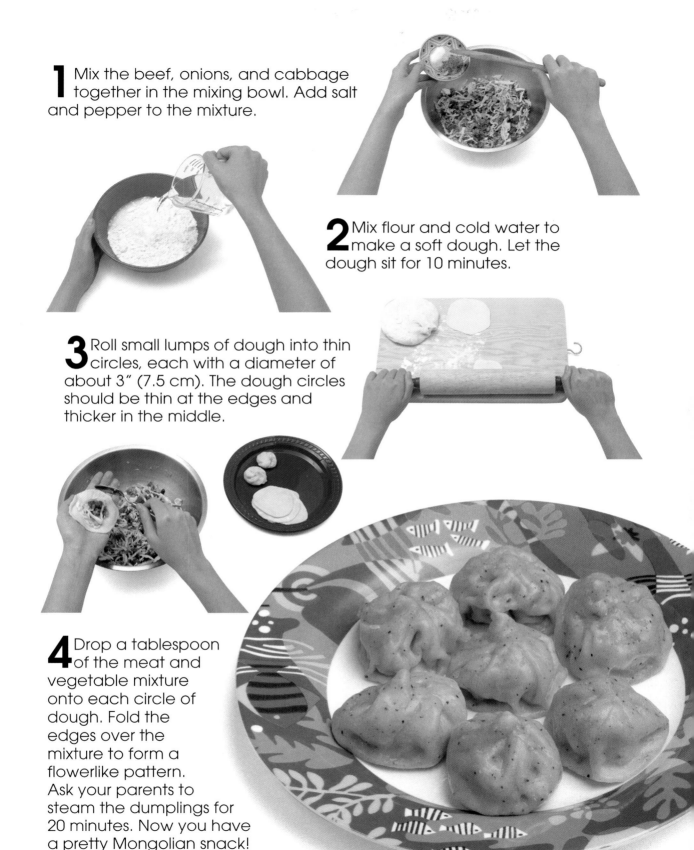

31

GLOSSARY

accomplished, 22	Highly skilled.
amenities, 16	Things that help make a person comfortable.
collapsible, 9	Can be taken apart easily.
dynamic, 25	Energetic.
existence, 10	A way of living.
independent republic, 4	A country with its own government elected by its own citizens.
inhabitants, 9	People or animals that live in a particular place.
invincibility, 22	A level of power that cannot be defeated.
lavish, 6	Very elaborate.
mime, 25	To perform through actions without words.
reincarnations, 15	The souls of people reborn after death in a new human body or some other living form.
triumph, 25	Victory or success.
virtues, 21	Good qualities or features.

INDEX

Picture credits
Camera Press: 7 (top), 8 (bottom), 9 (bottom), 18, 19, 23 (bottom), 28; David Edwards: 1, 3 (top), 4, 9 (top), 10 (top), 13, 17 (bottom), 20 (top); Haga Library: 16, 20 (bottom), 21 (bottom), 24, 25 (top); HBL Network Photo Agency: 2, 8 (top), 12, 14 (bottom), 17 (top), 25 (bottom); Hutchison Library: 10 (bottom), 14 (top), 22 (top); Trip Photographic Library: 5, 15, 22 (bottom), 23 (top), 26; Nik Wheeler: 3 (bottom), 6, 7 (bottom), 11 (both), 21 (top)

Digital scanning by Superskill Graphics Pte Ltd.